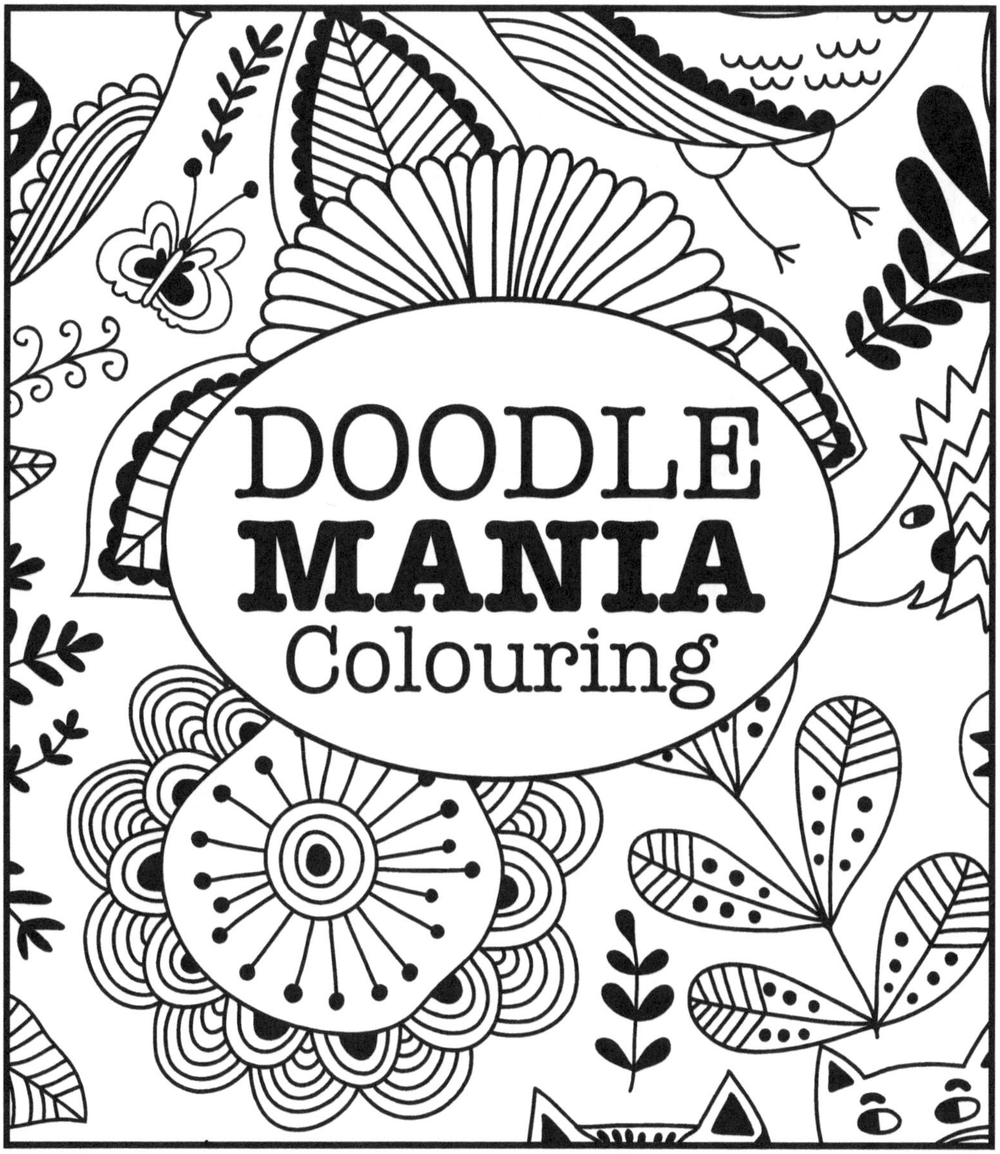

DOODLE MANIA Colouring

Gorgeous Colouring For Girls **Book 4**

First published in 2016 by Kyle Craig Publishing

Design: Elizabeth James, Julie Anson, Alison McNicol, Shutterstock, Inc.

ISBN: 978-1-78595-121-3

A CIP record for this book is available from the British Library.

A Kyle Craig Publication

www.kyle-craig.com

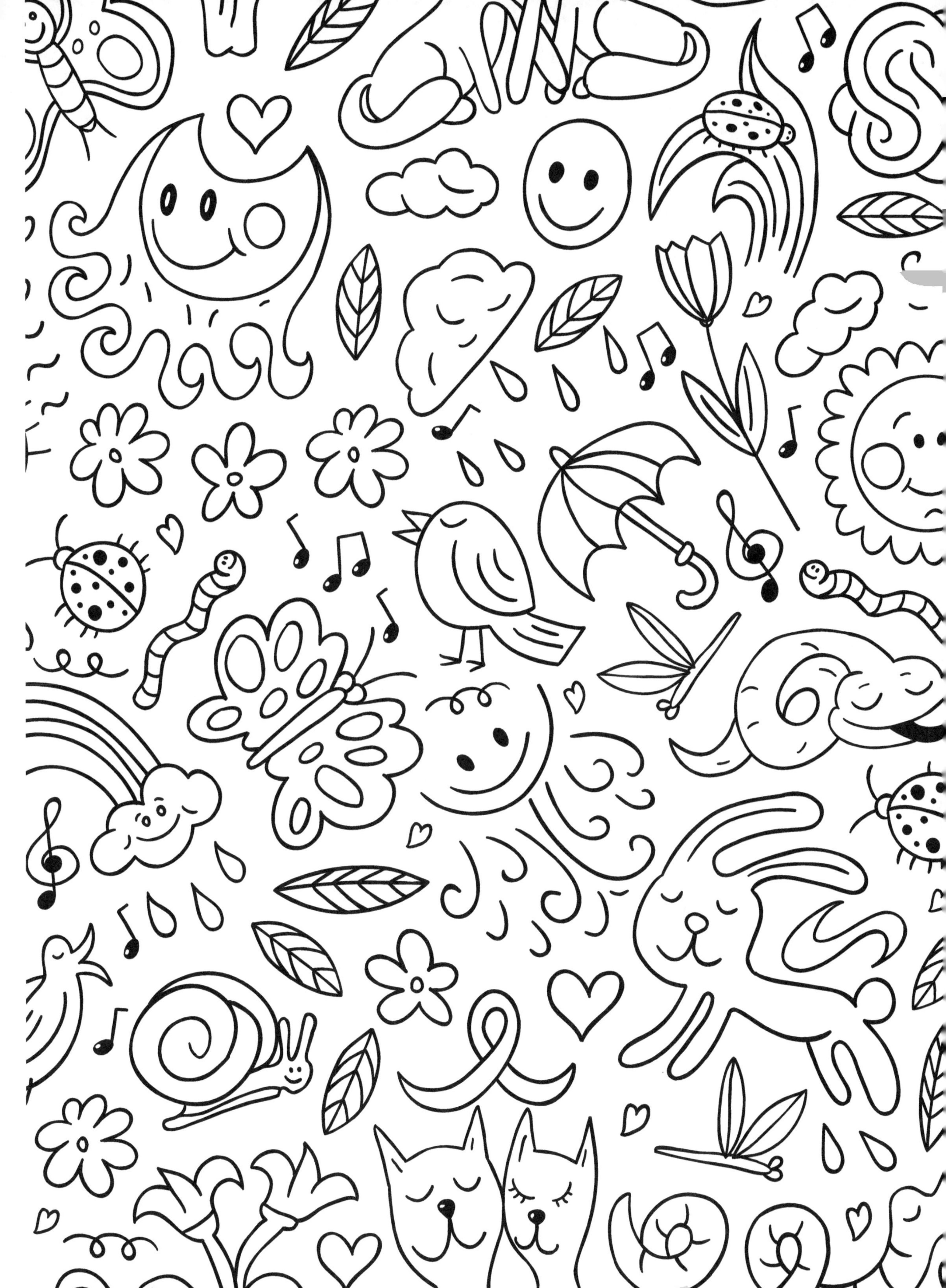

HAPPY
BIRTHDAY
POP
CORN
CHOKO

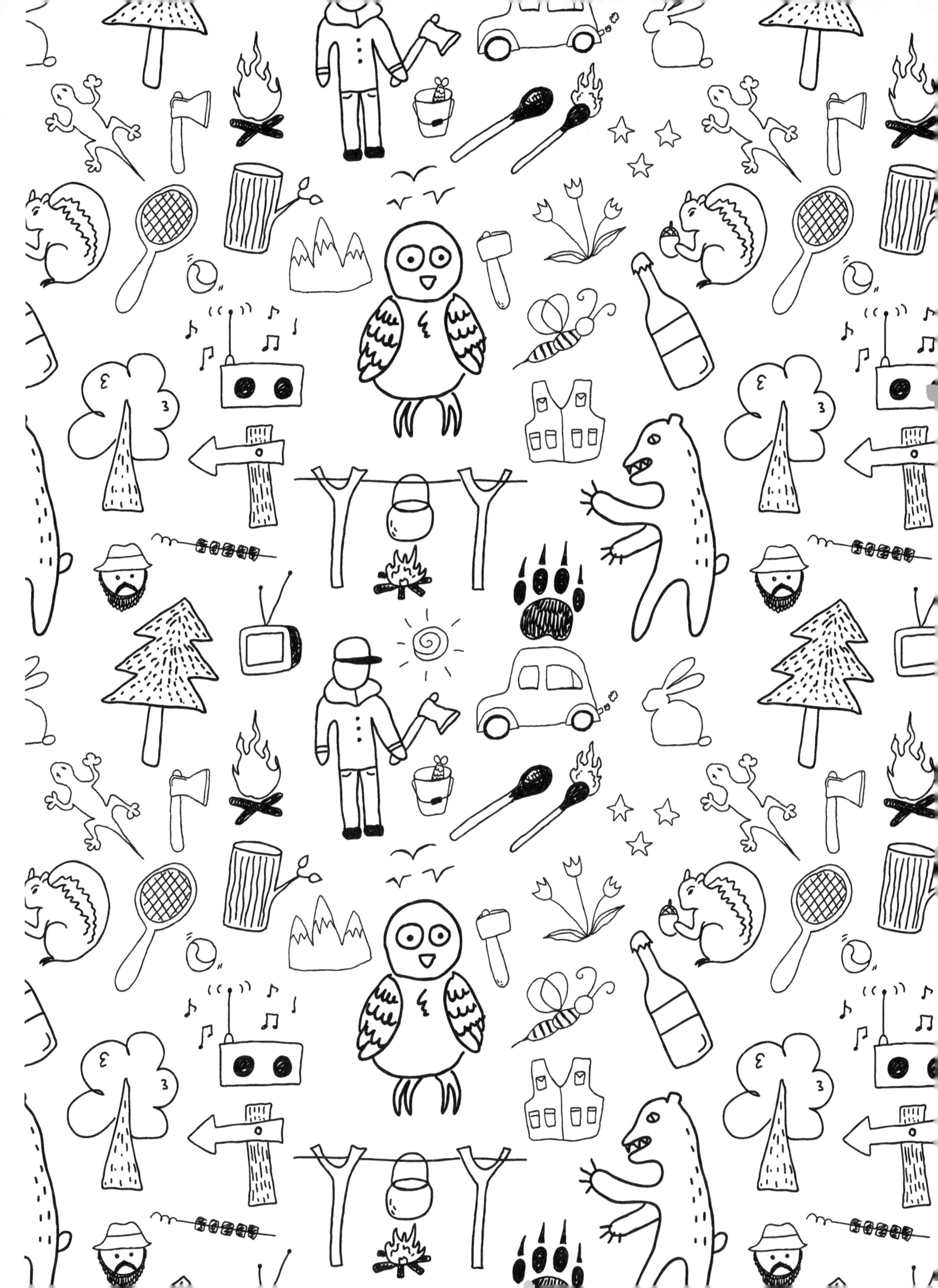

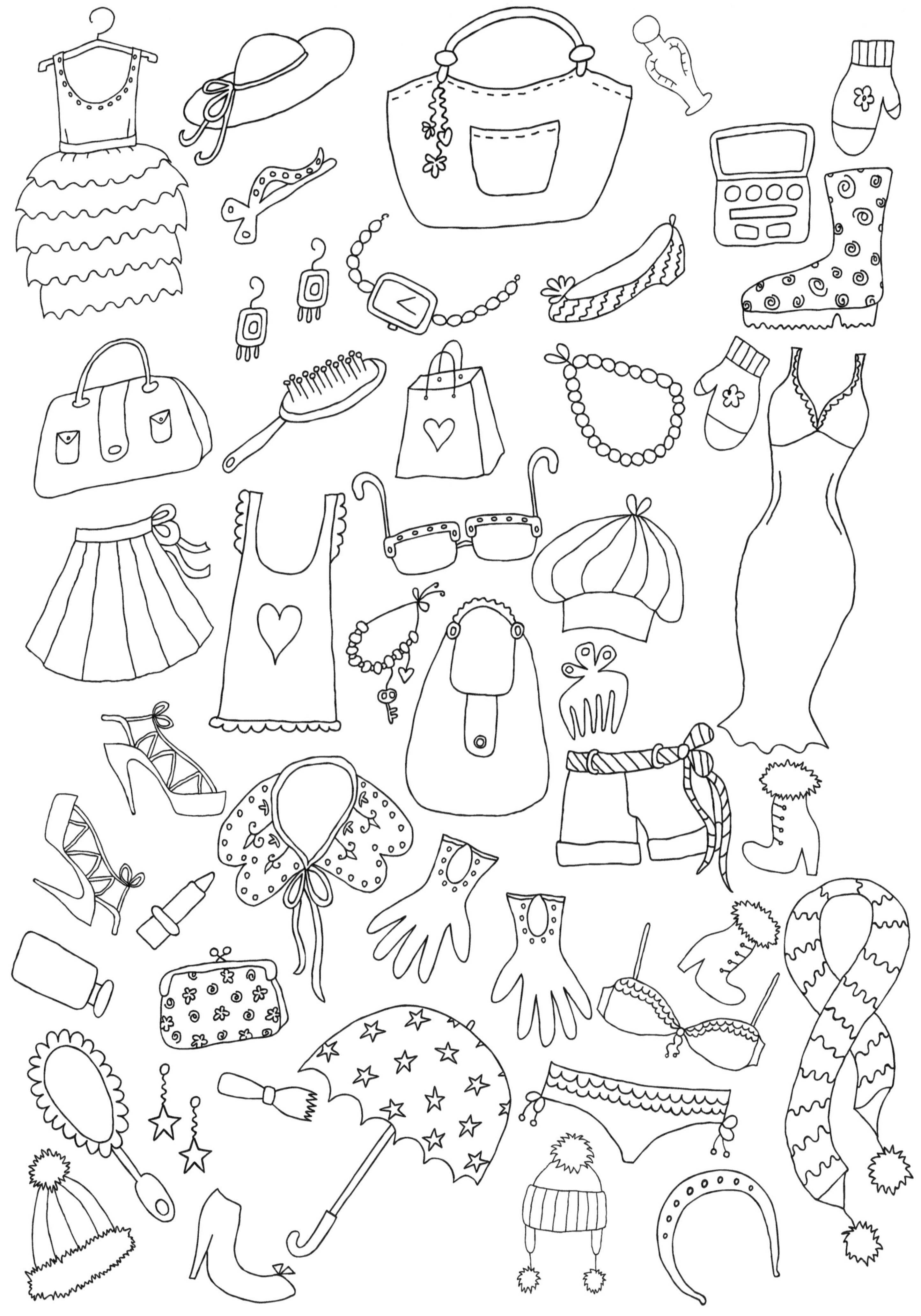

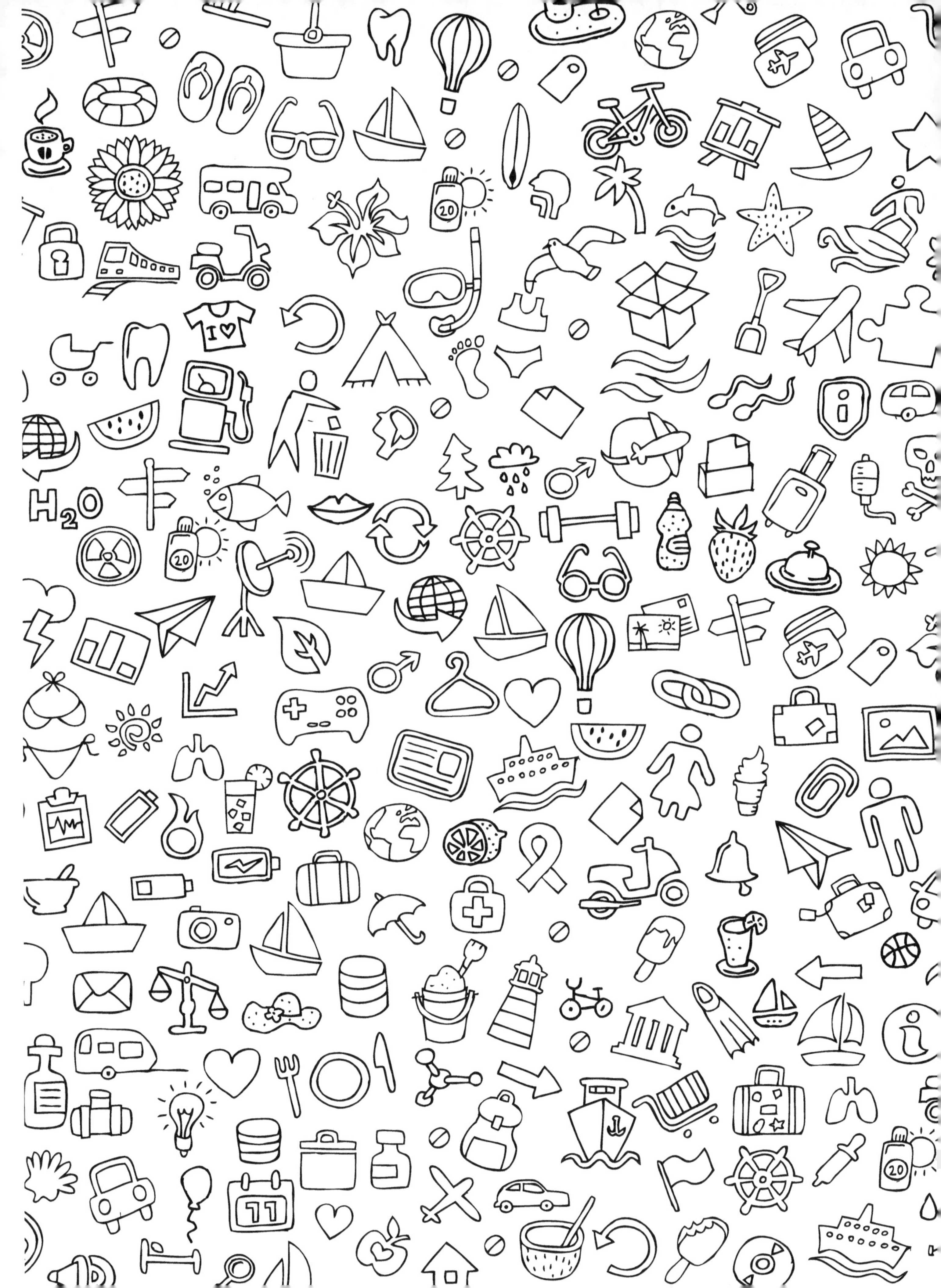
H2O
I
20
20
20
11

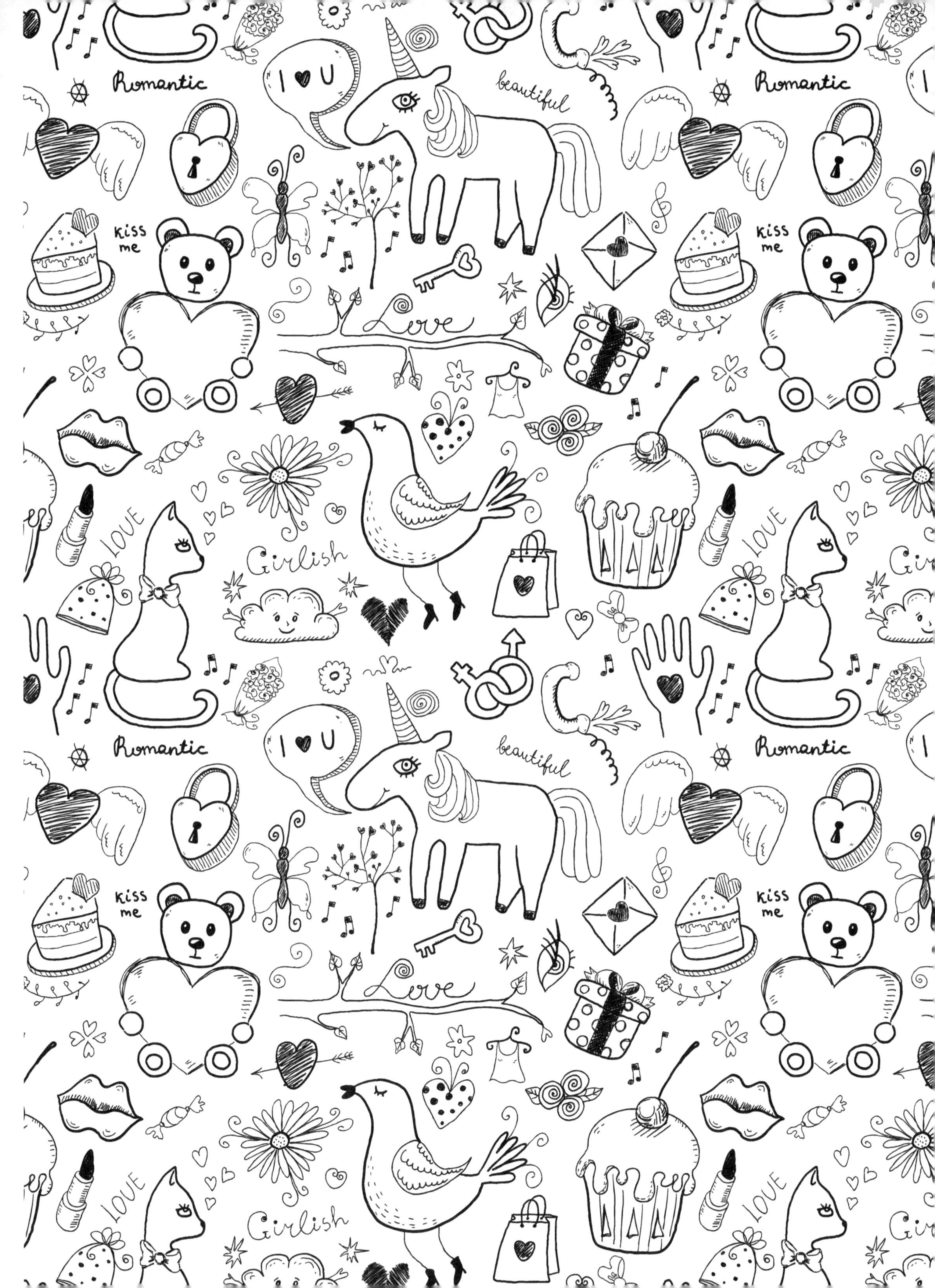
Romantic
I ♥ U
beautiful
Romantic
kiss me
kiss me
Love
LOVE
Girlish
LOVE
Romantic
I ♥ U
beautiful
Romantic
kiss me
kiss me
Love
LOVE
Girlish
LOVE

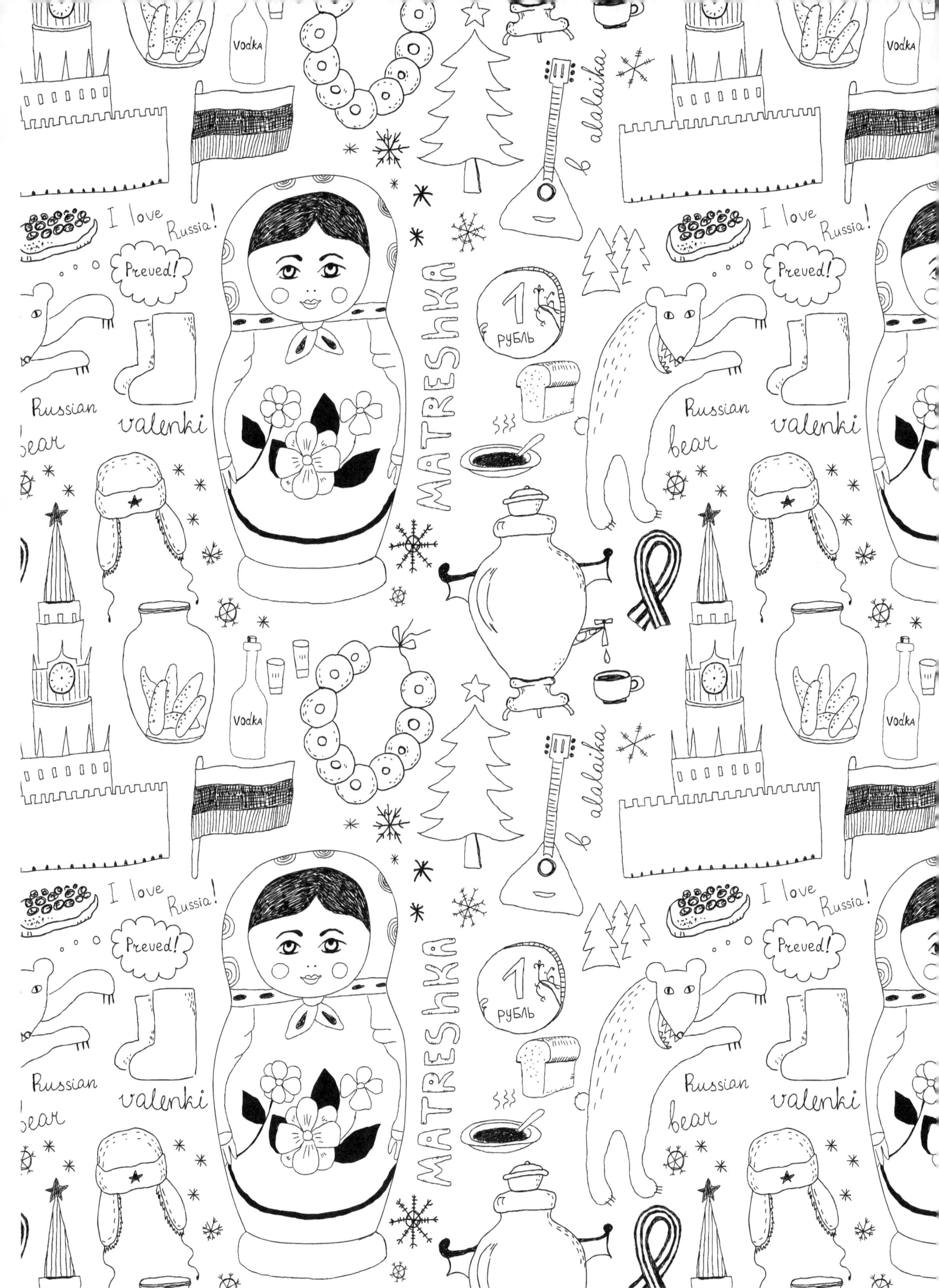
Vodka
I love Russia!
Preved!
Russian bear
valenki
MATRESHKA
Balalaika
1 РУБЛЬ

Hi!
Hi!
Hi!
Hi!

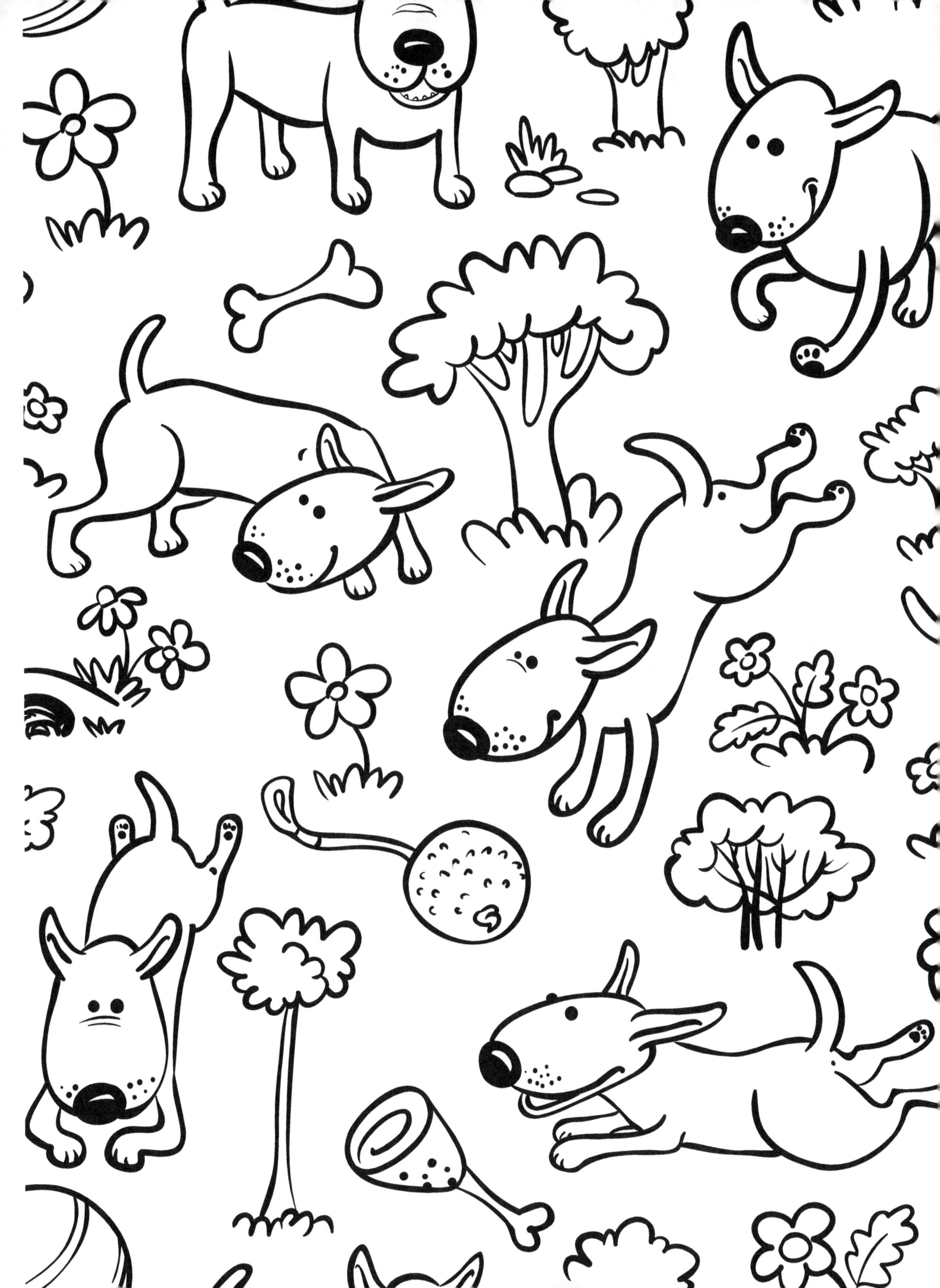

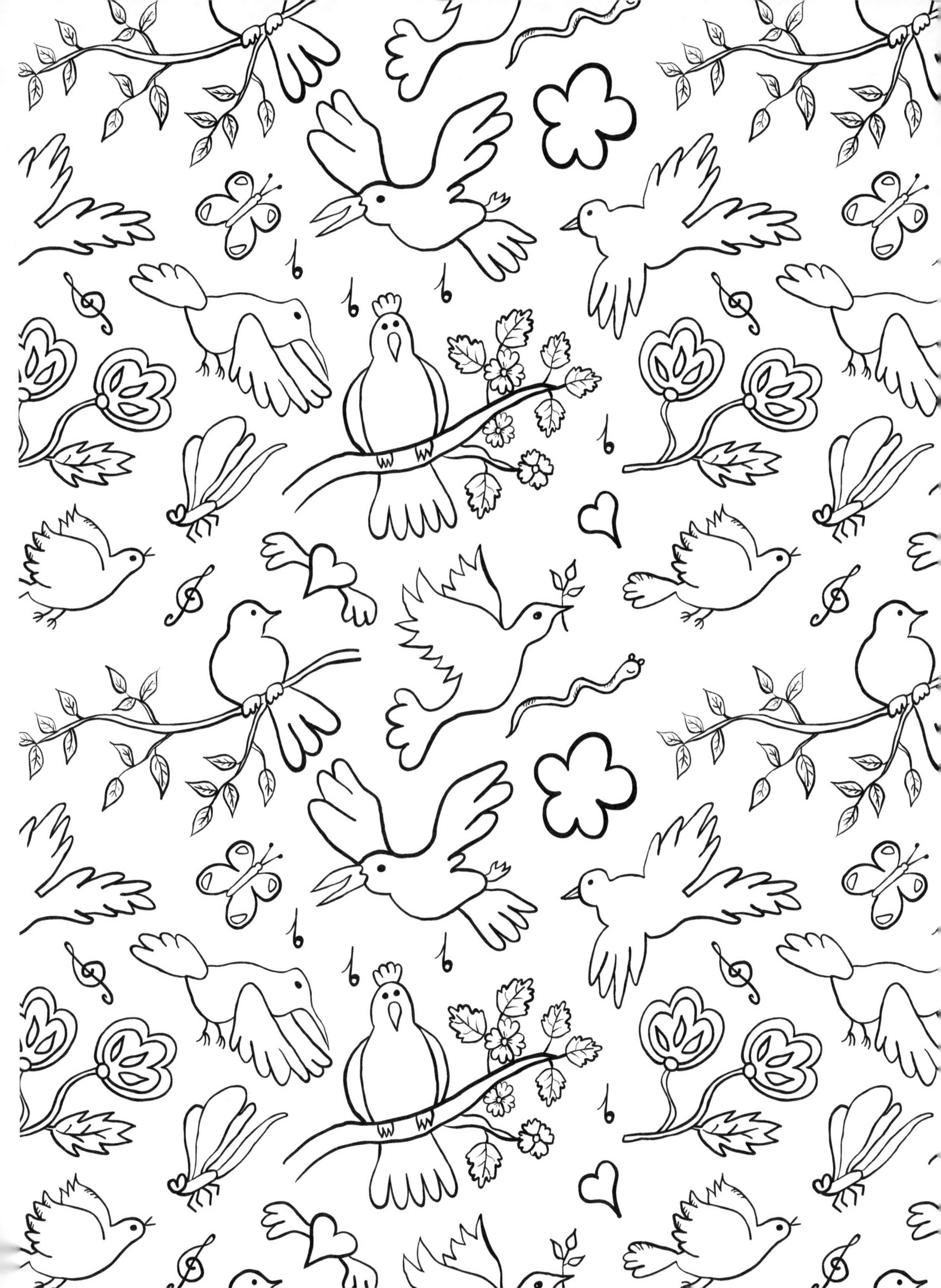

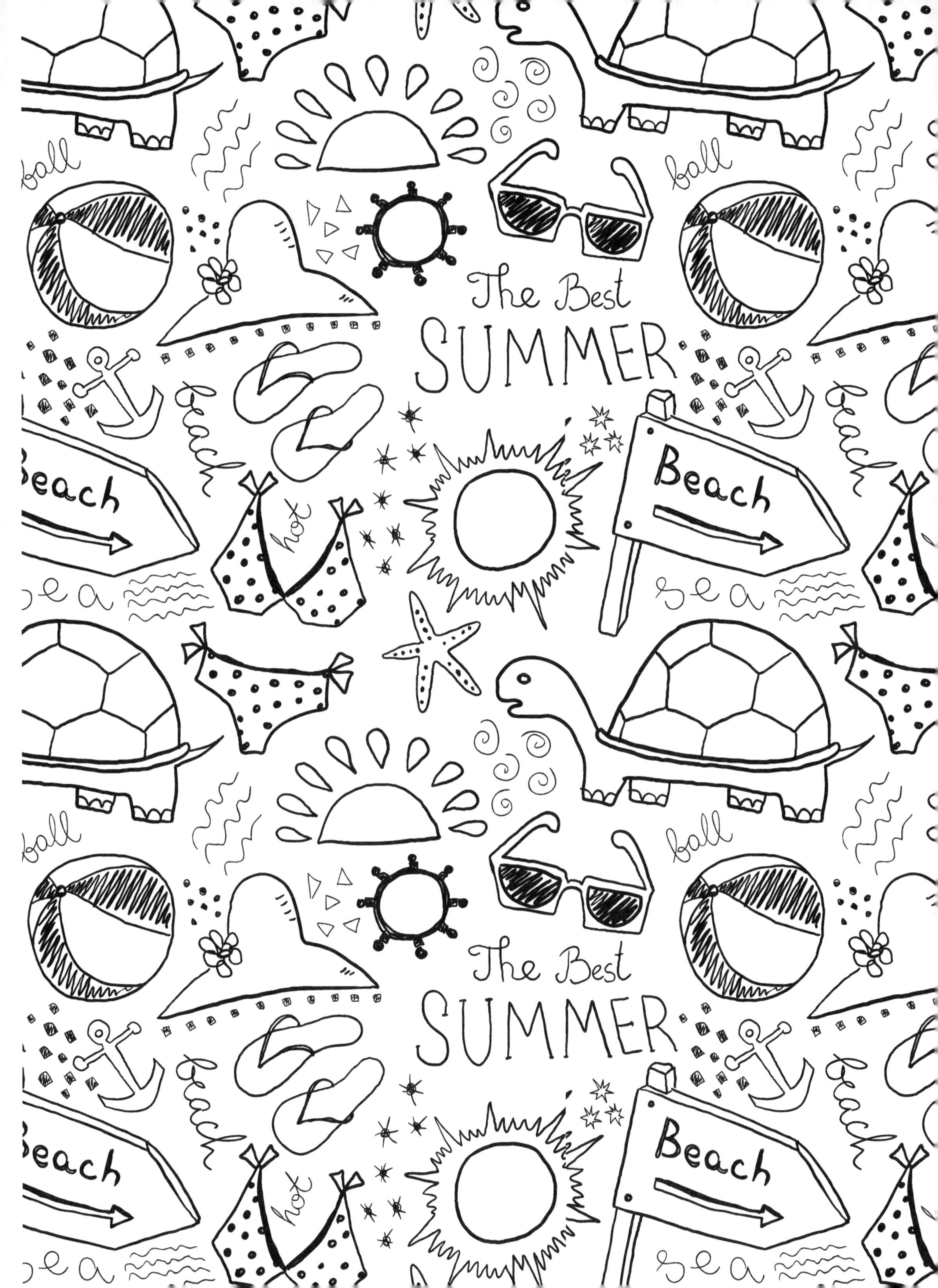
ball
The Best
SUMMER
beach
Beach
hot
sea
ball
The Best
SUMMER
beach
Beach
hot
sea

LOVE
LOVE

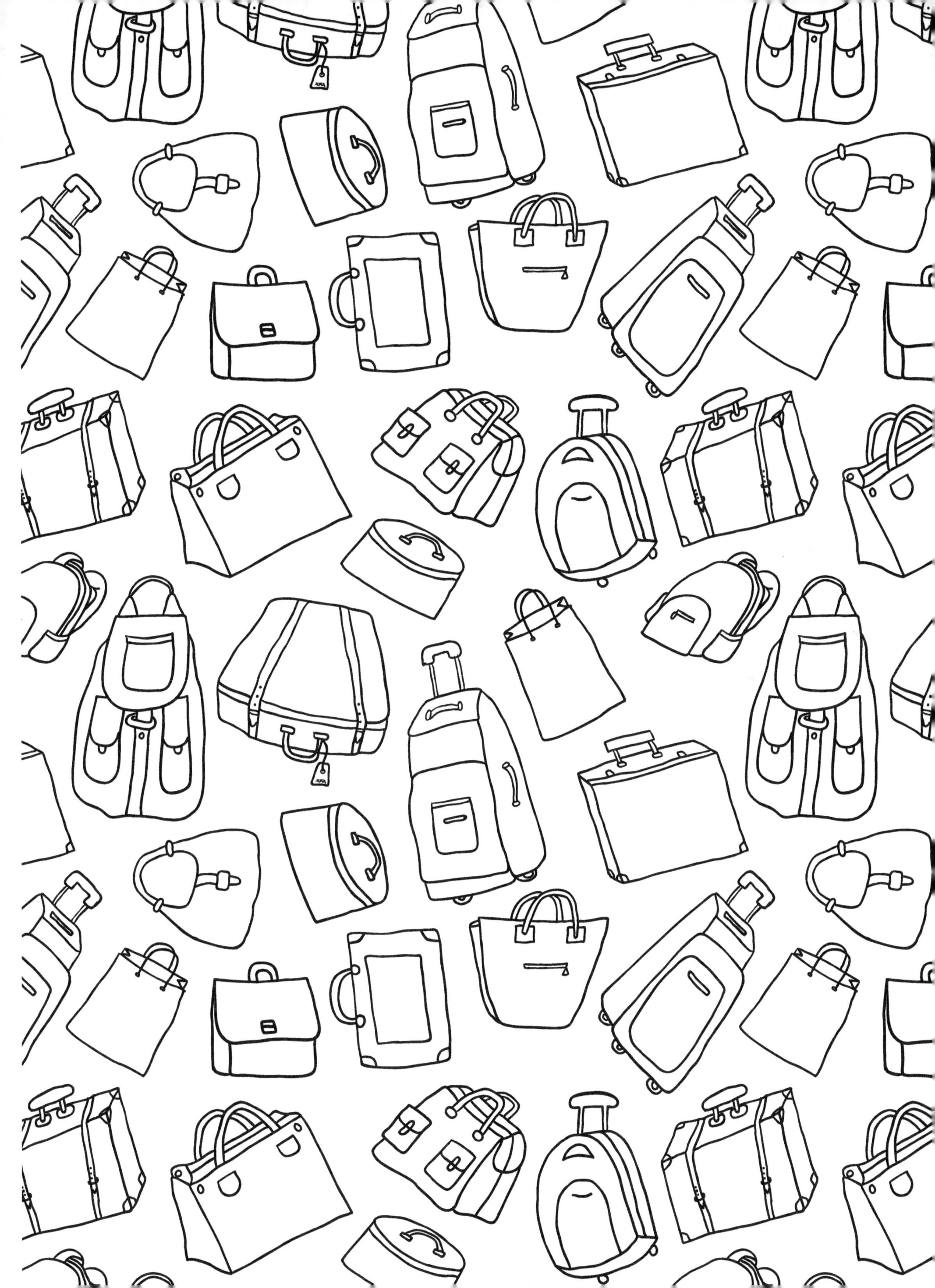

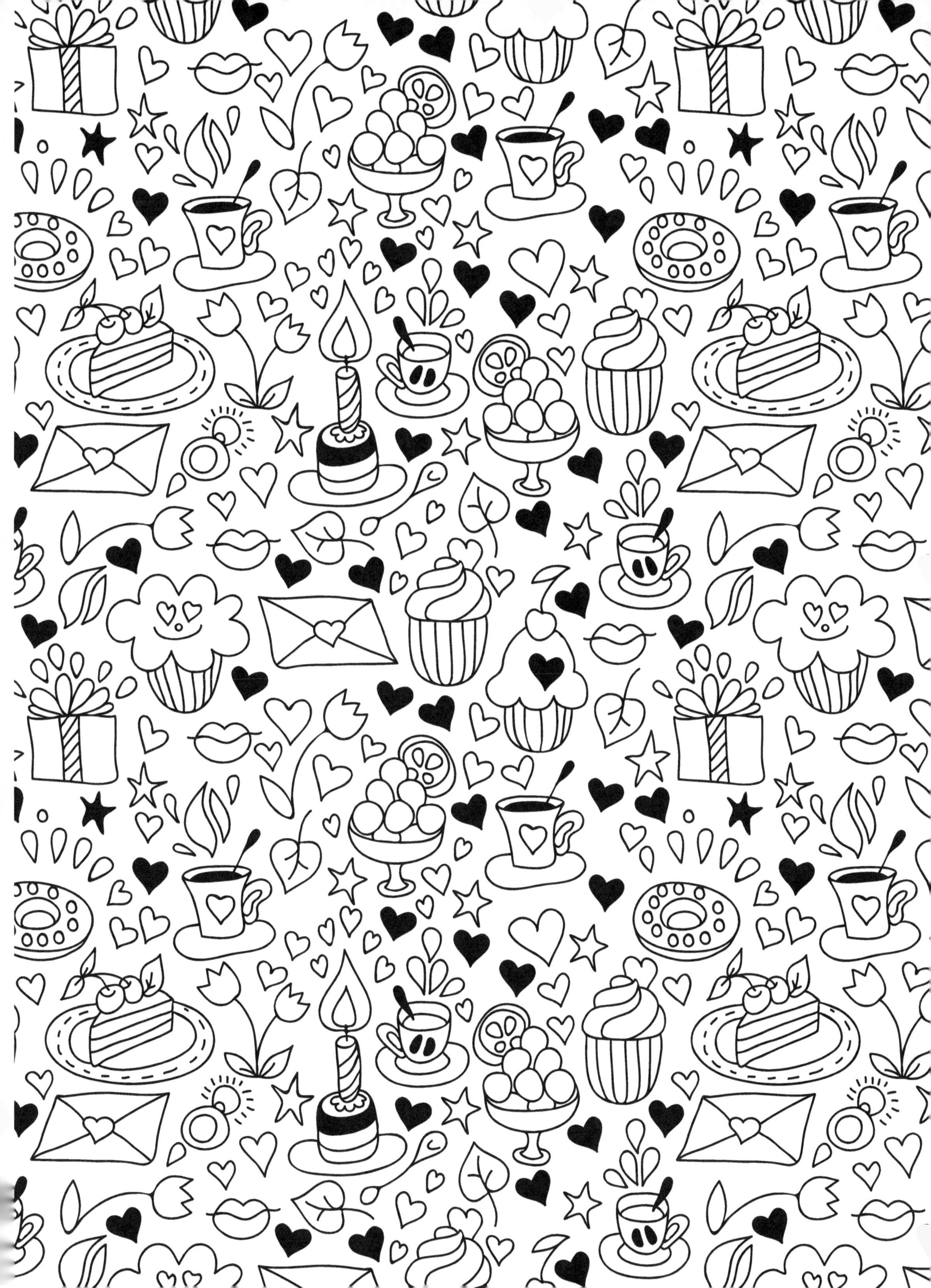

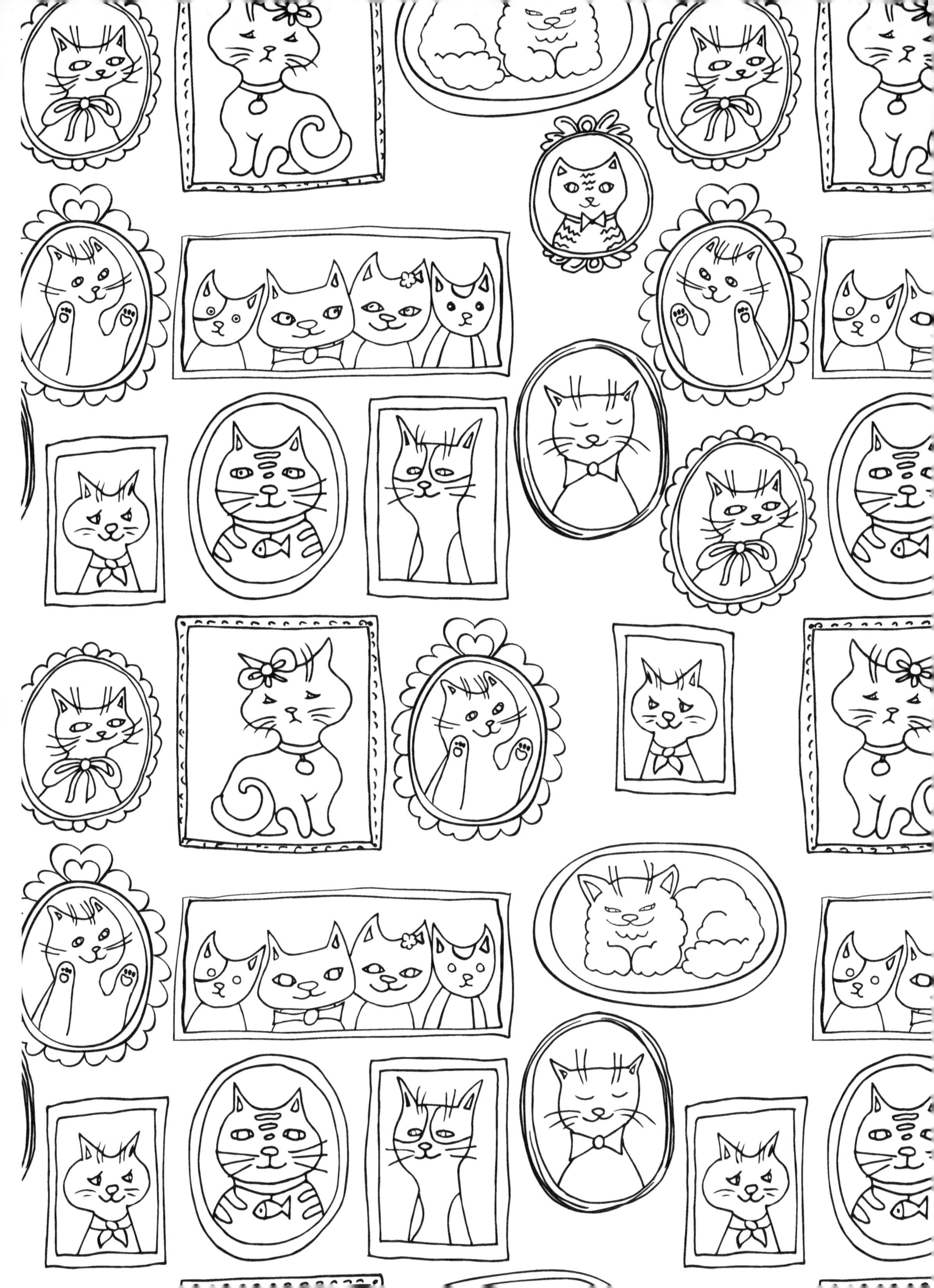

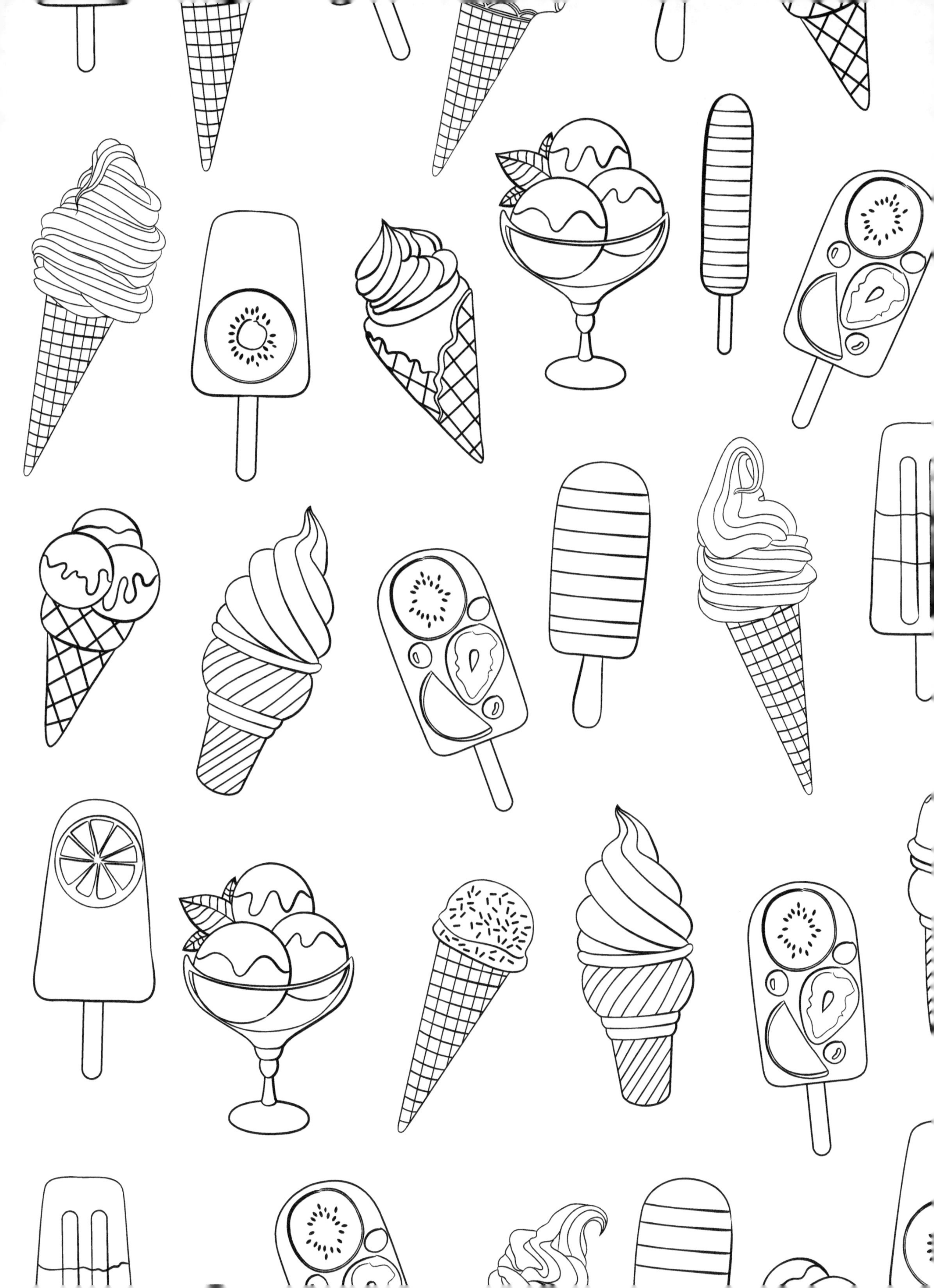

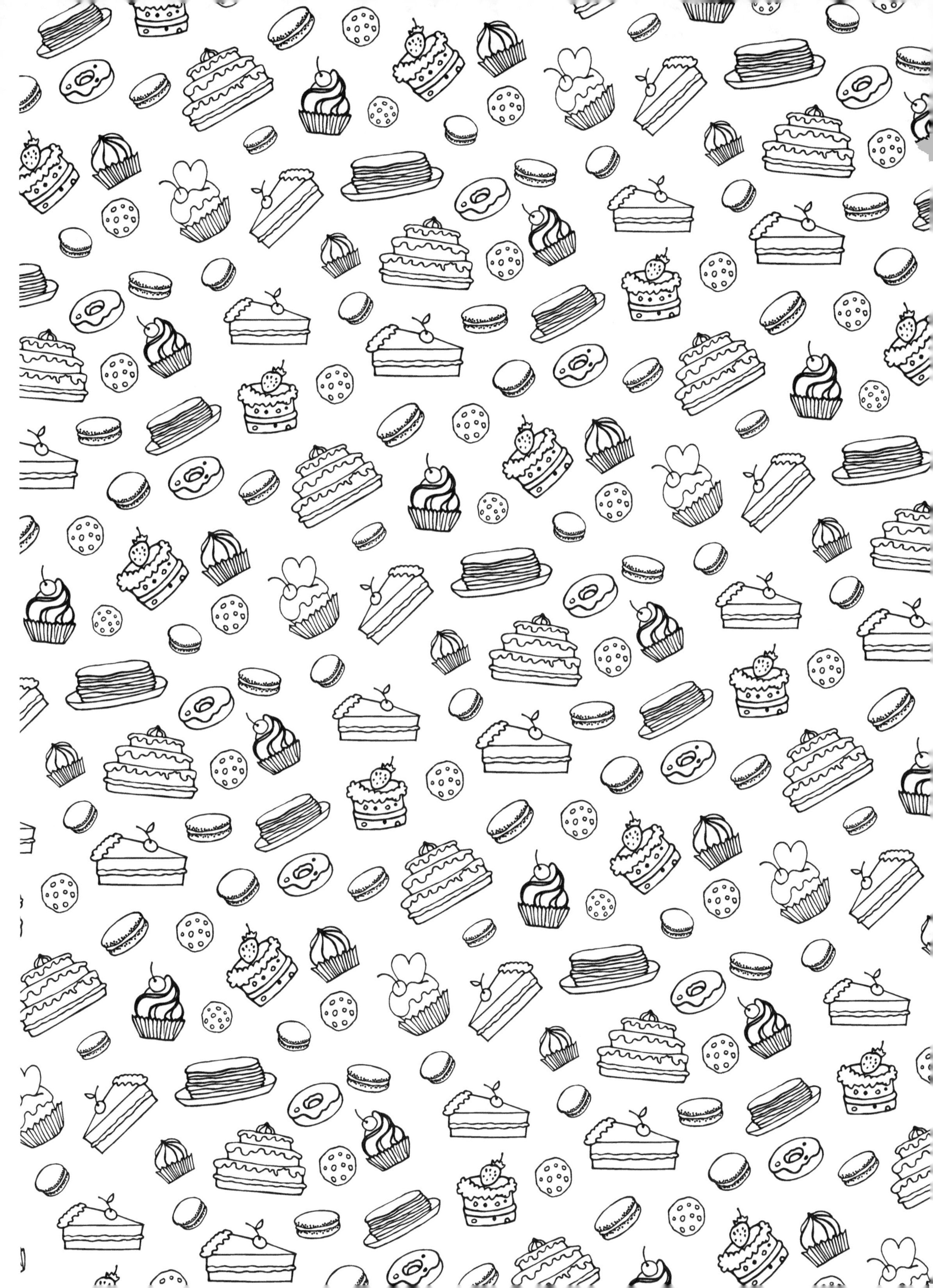

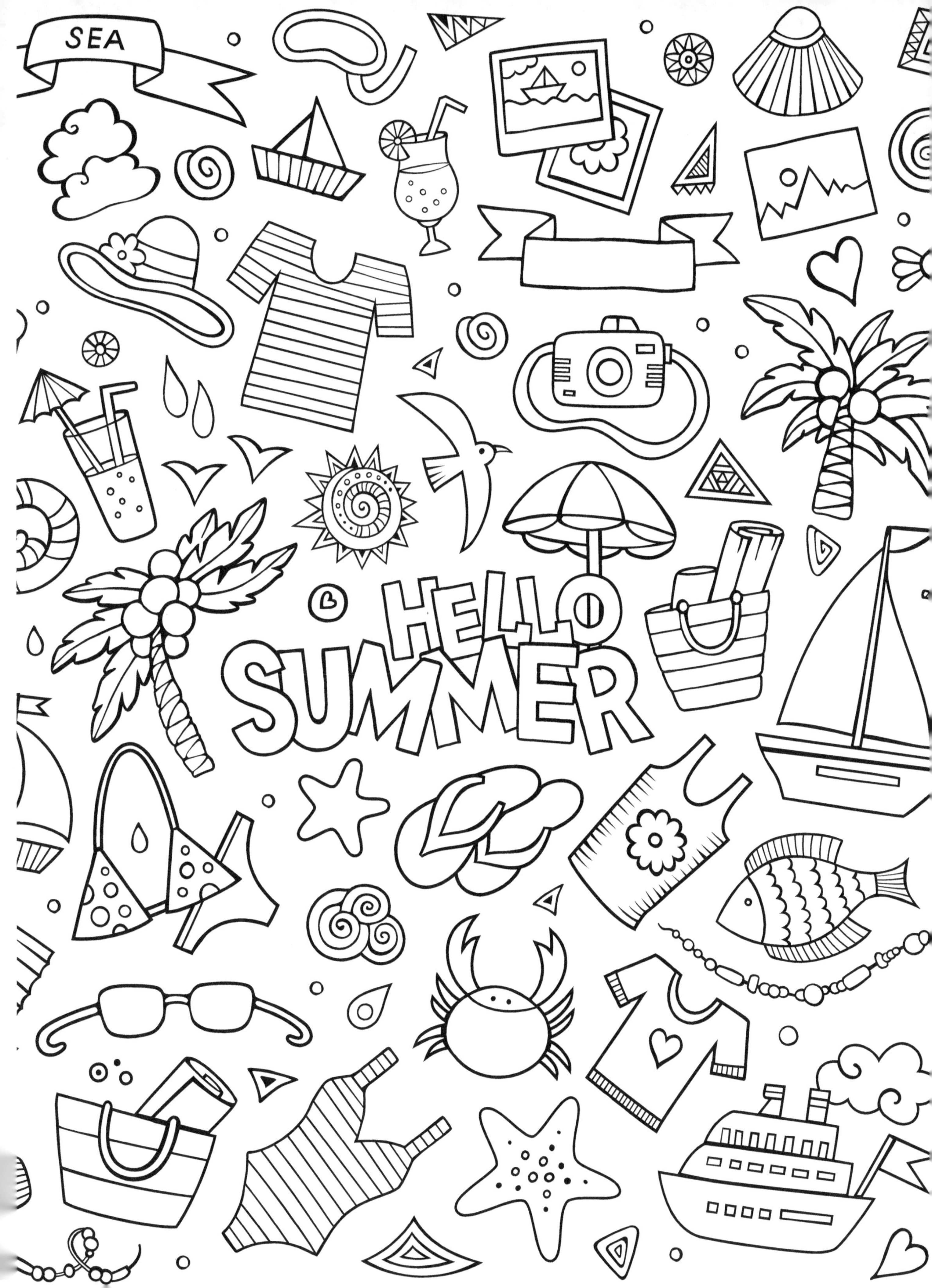
SEA
HELLO
SUMMER

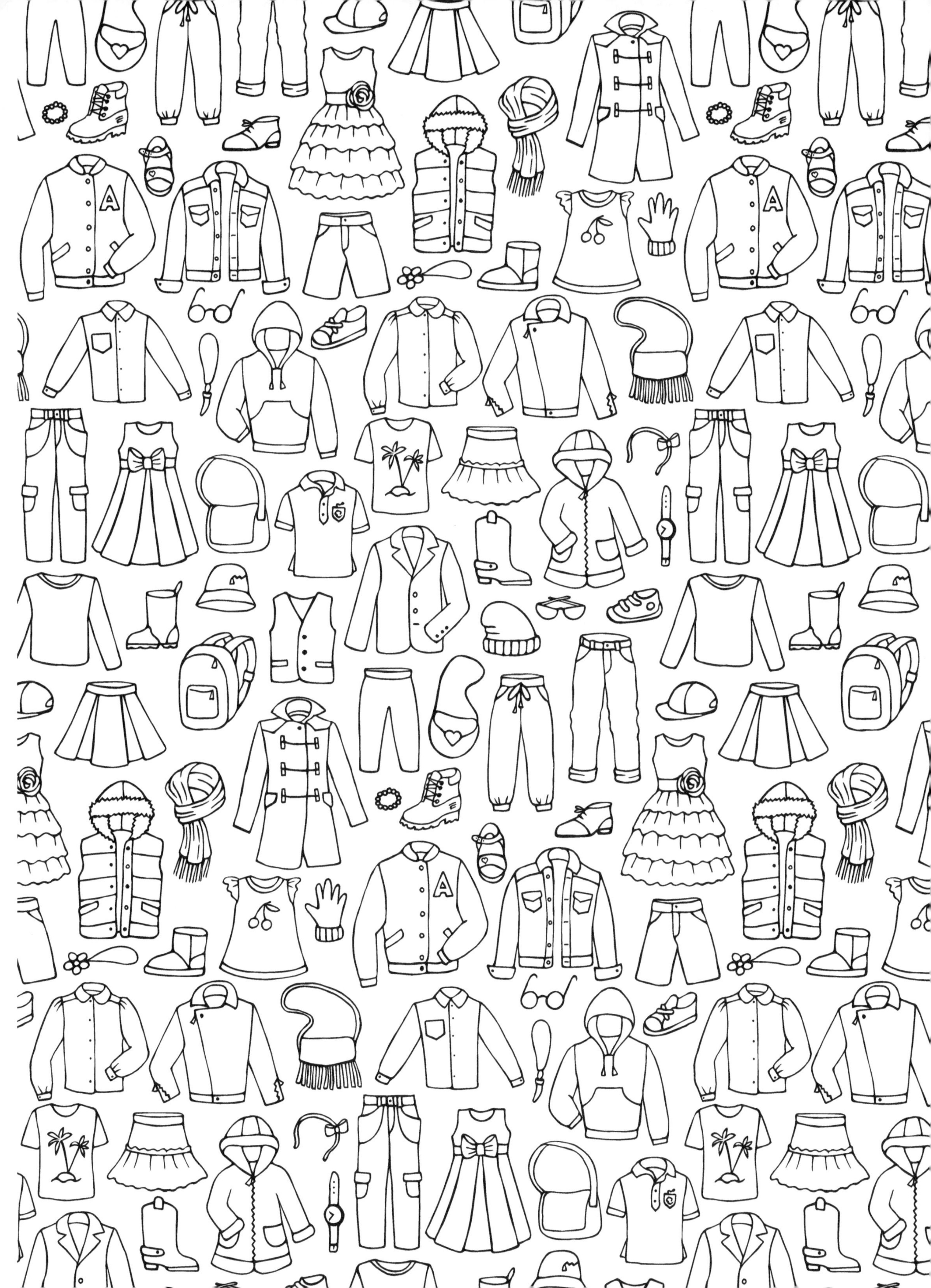

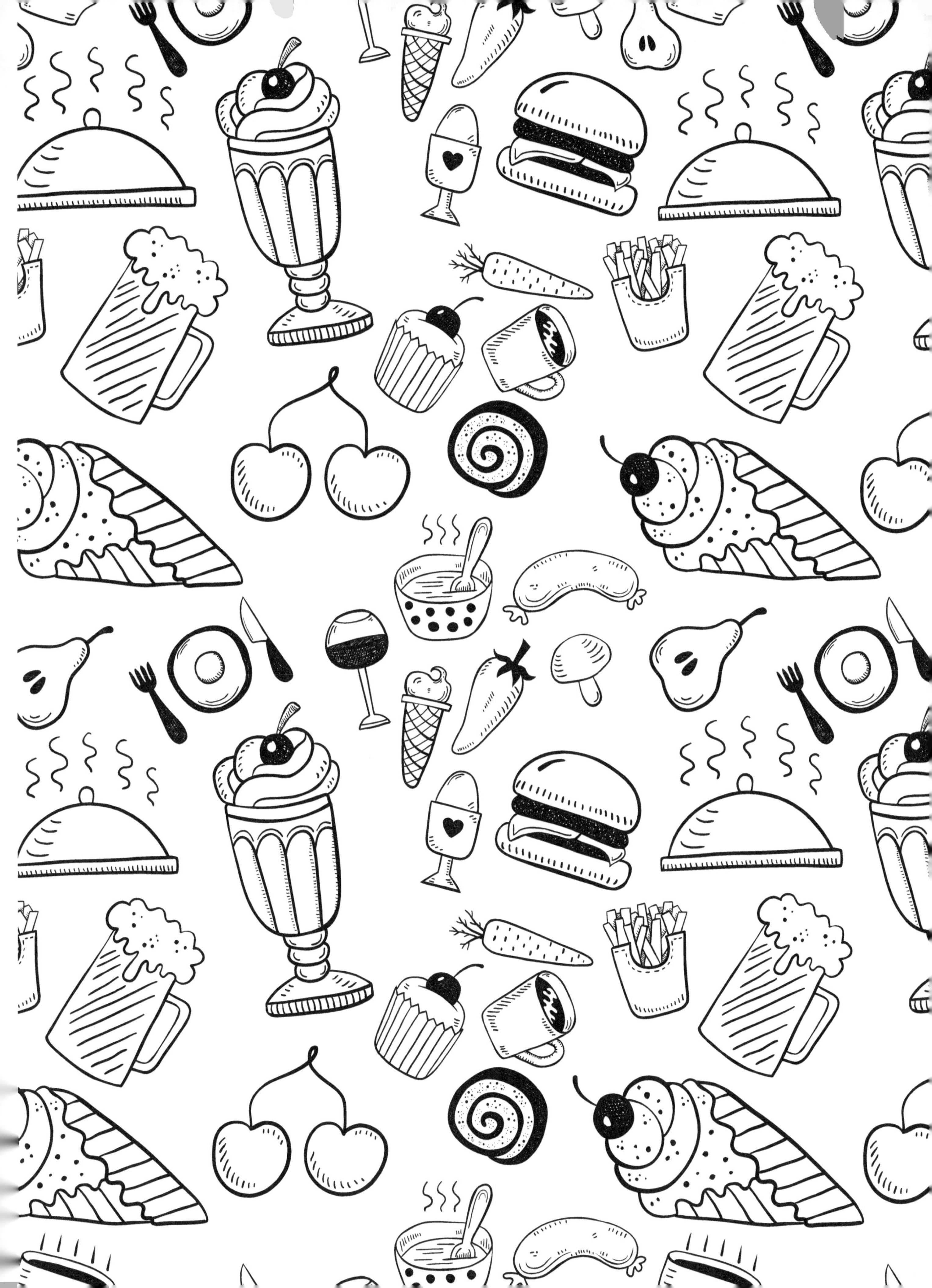

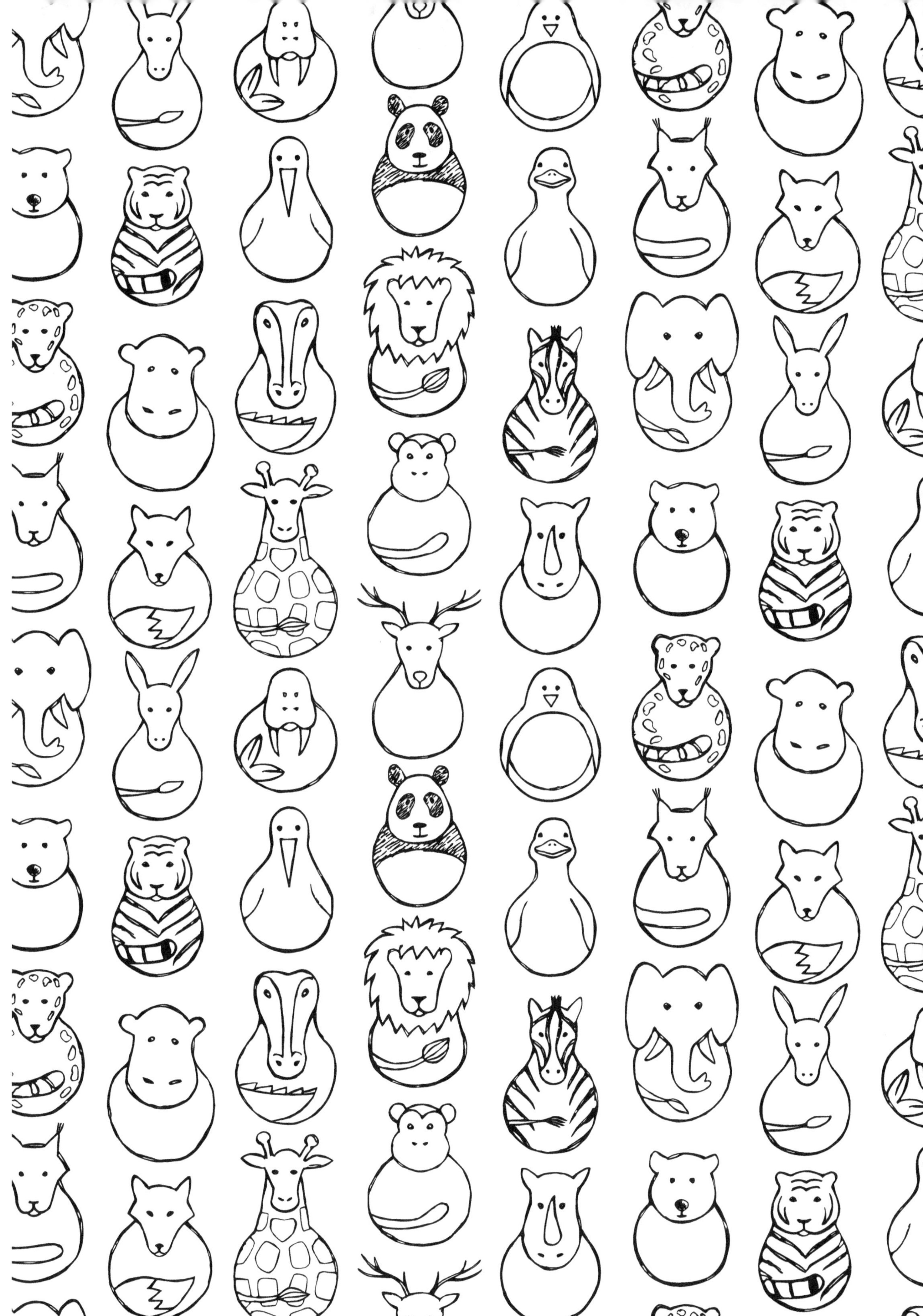

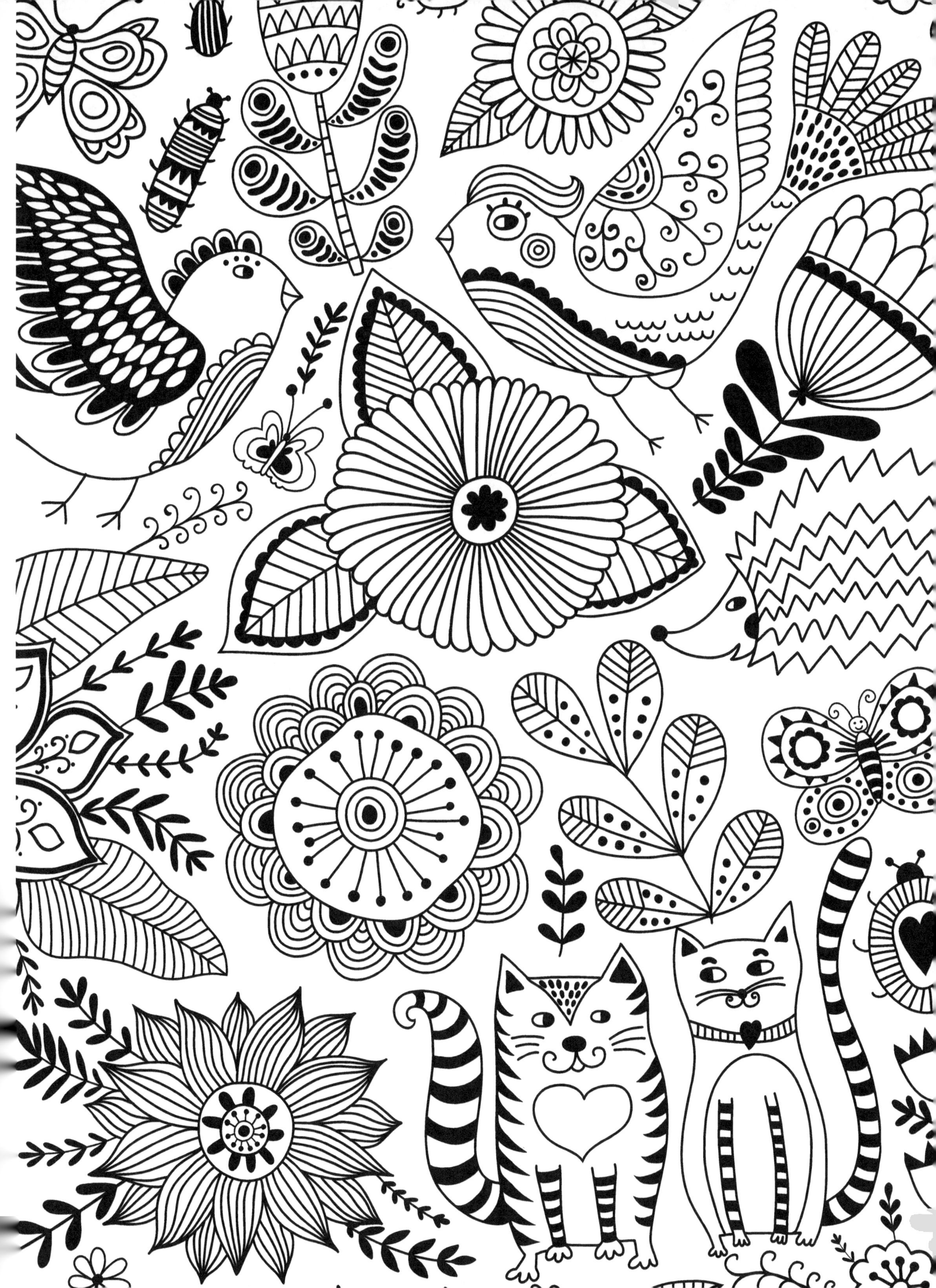

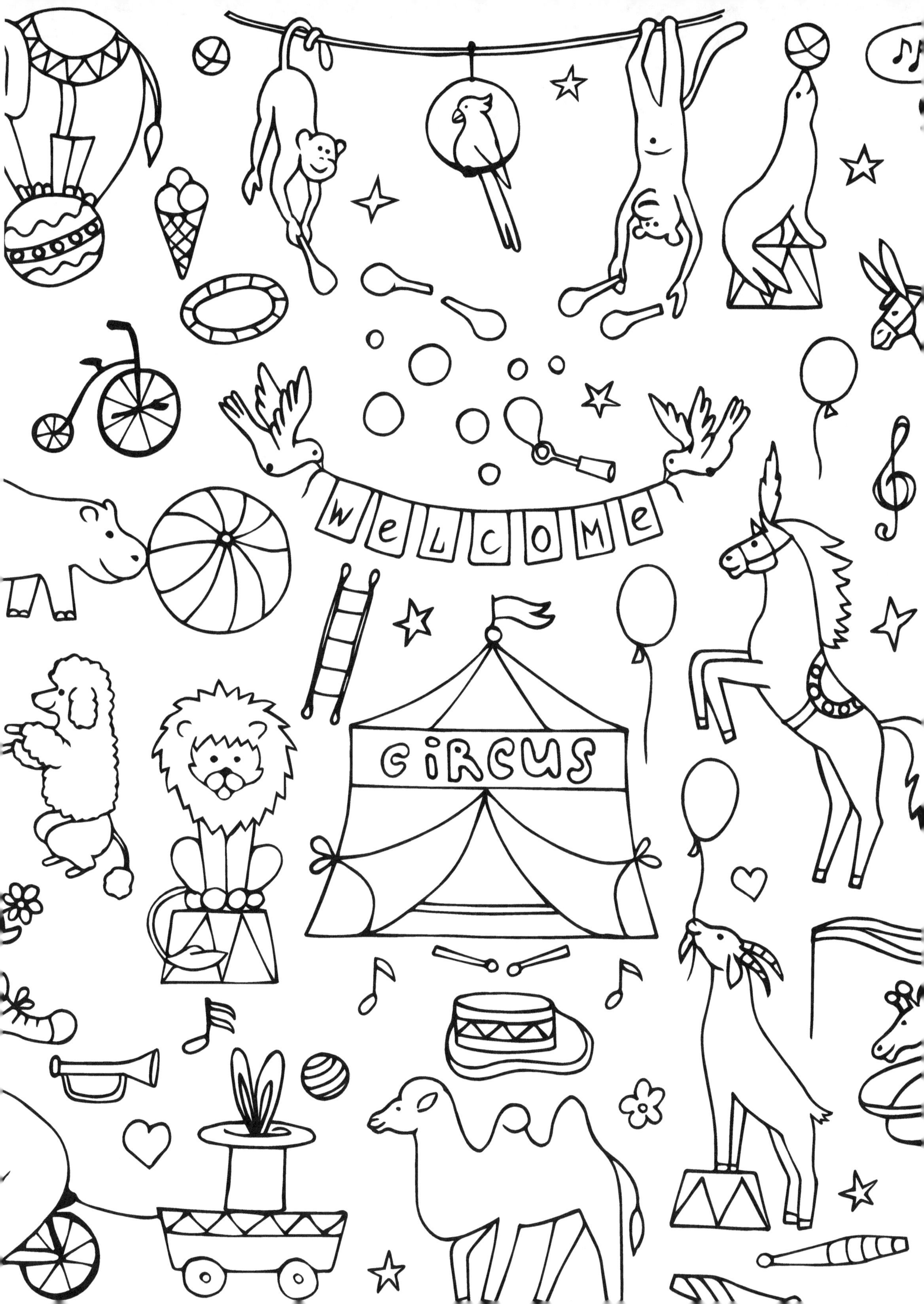
WELCOME
CIRCUS

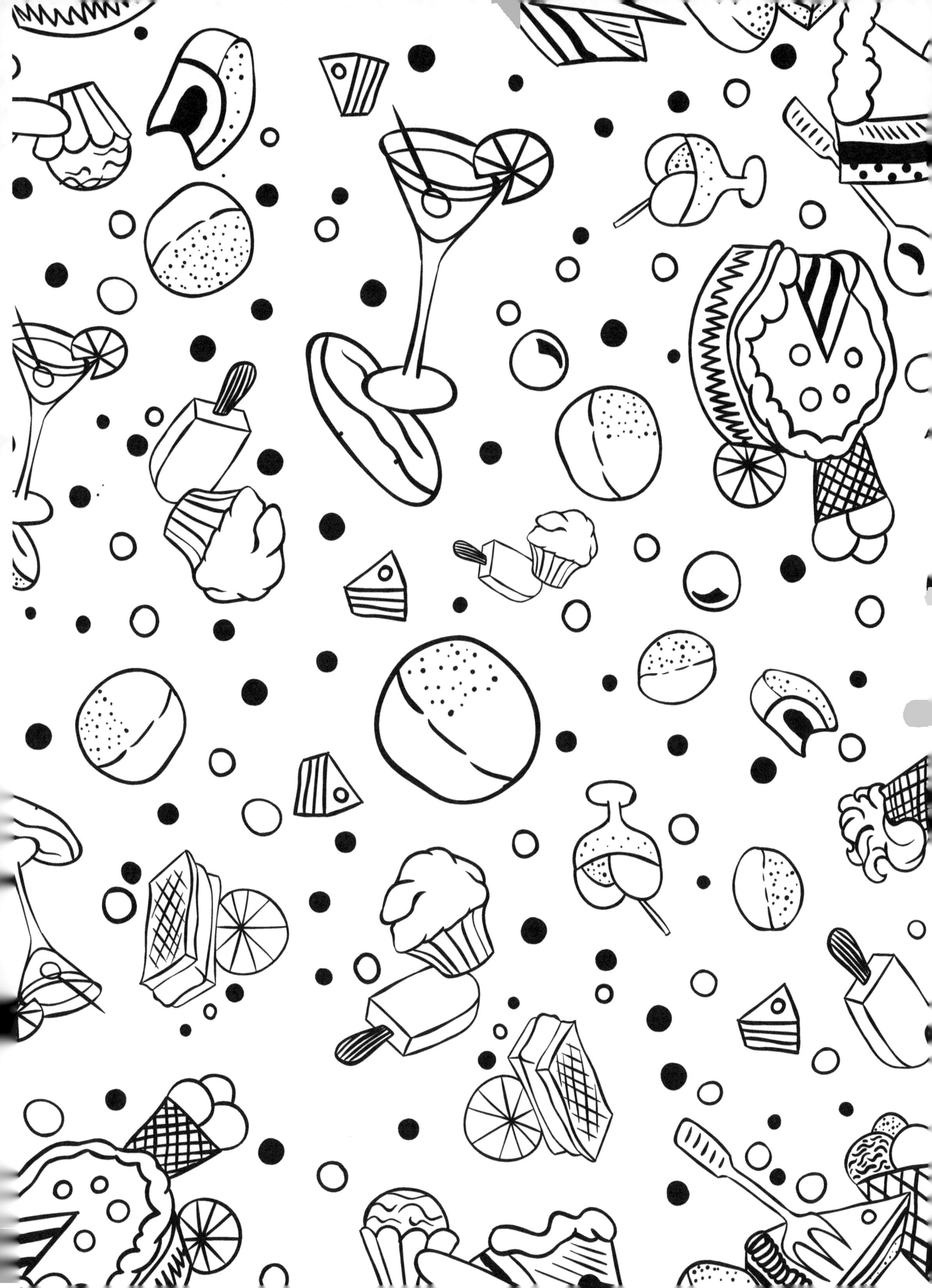

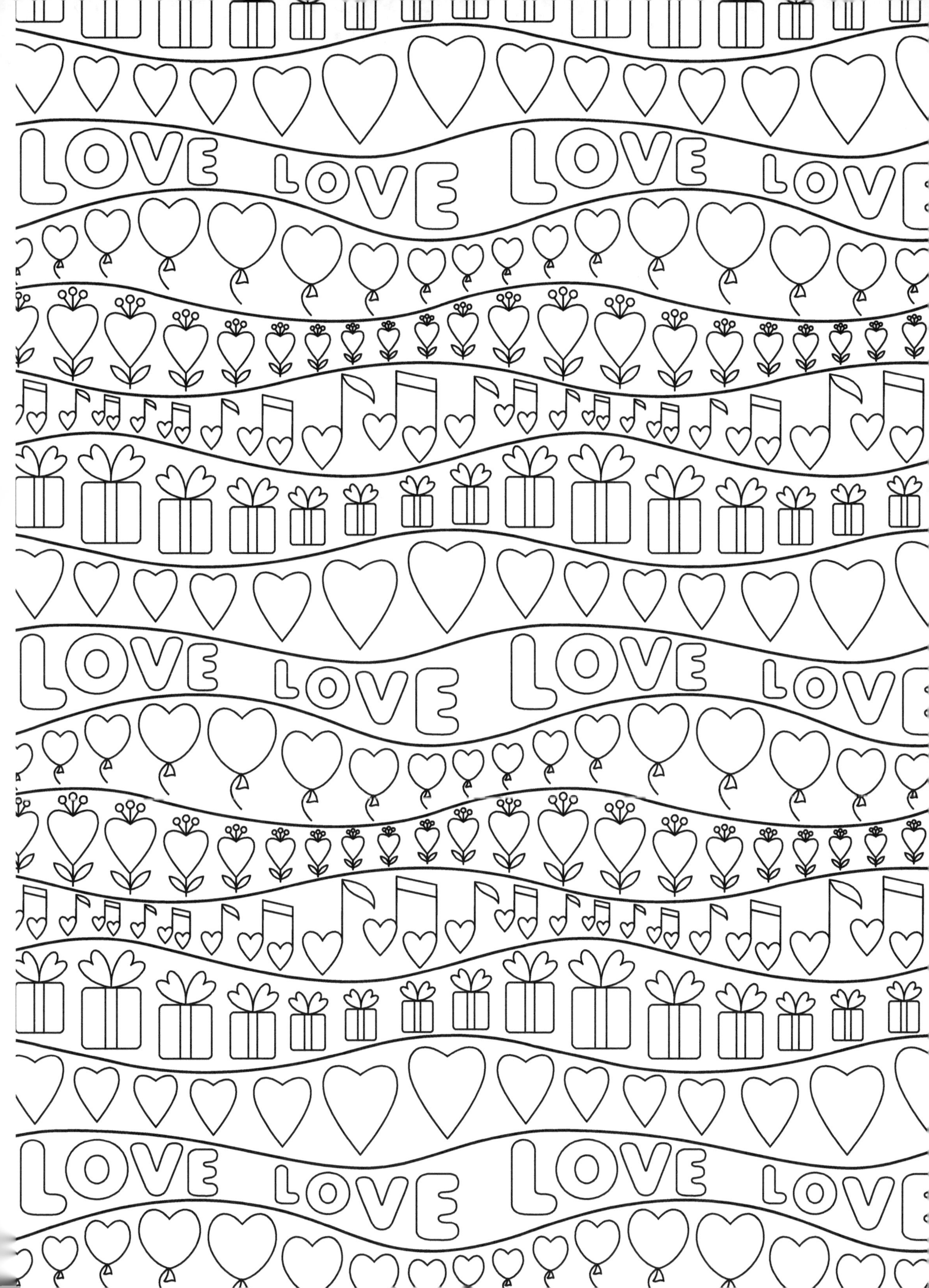
LOVE
LOVE
LOVE
LOVE
LOVE
LOVE
LOVE
LOVE
LOVE

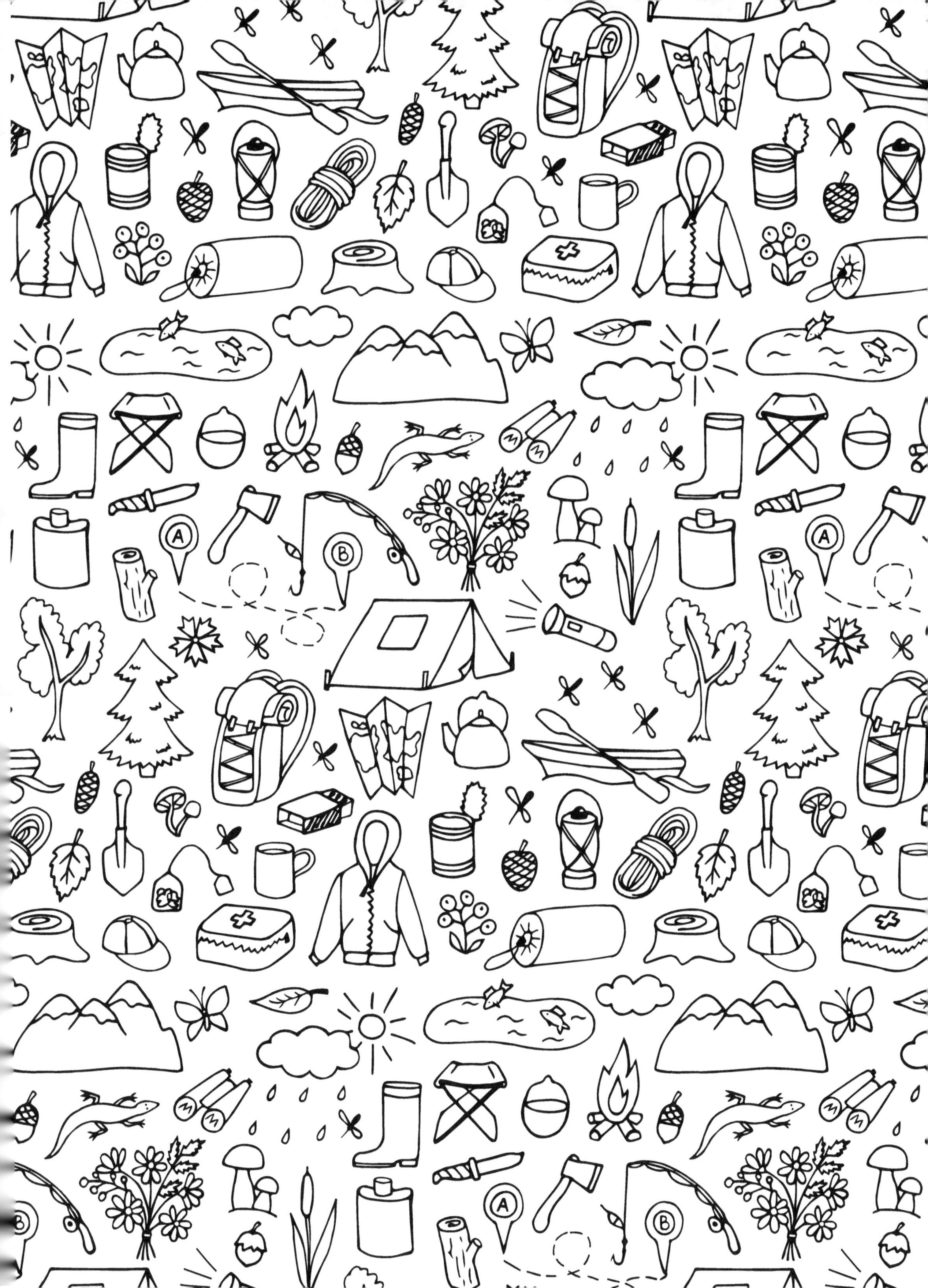

A
B

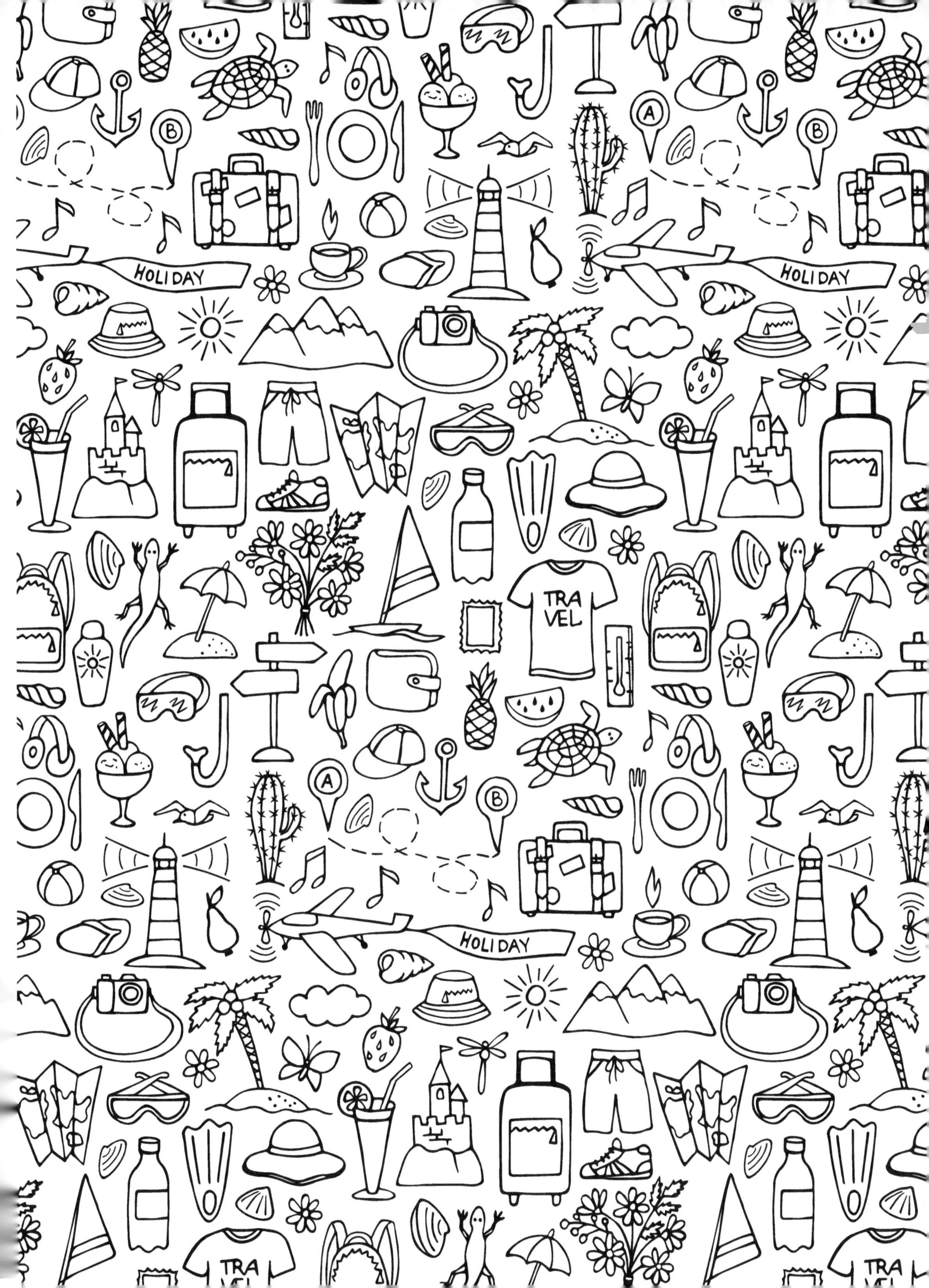
HOLIDAY
HOLIDAY
TRA VEL
TRA VEL
HOLIDAY
TRA VEL
TRA VEL

www.ingramcontent.com/pod-product-compliance
Lightning Source LLC
La Vergne TN
LVHW061255100826
845148LV00008B/1134

9781785951213